Beautiful Pressure

Beautiful Pressure

Jay Couture

Copyright © 2010 by Jay Couture.

Library of Congress Control Number: 2010903672
ISBN: Hardcover   978-1-4500-6298-5
                   Softcover   978-1-4500-6297-8
                   E-book   978-1-4500-6299-2

All rights reserved. No part of this book may be reproduced or transmitted in any form or by any means, electronic or mechanical, including photocopying, recording, or by any information storage and retrieval system, without permission in writing from the copyright owner.

This book was printed in the United States of America.

To order additional copies of this book, contact:
Xlibris Corporation
1-888-795-4274
www.Xlibris.com
Orders@Xlibris.com
77661

CONTENTS

Beautiful Pressure 9
Good Morning 11
Goode Food for Thought 12
Disconnected 13
Gravity 14
Priceless 15
To Whom it may Concern 16
I got so Much Better 17
My Friends Say 18
I Love You 19
Who am I? 20
Broken Thermometer 21
The In-Crowd 22
He Said She Said 23
Circus in Brooklyn 25
Mr. East Meets West 26
First Aid Kit for Daughters 27
Cranberry Juice and Grey Goose 28
Men's fitting room 29
Beautiful 30
Big Brother 31
Proud Son 32
Pain 33
Dumb It Down 34
Miss the Good Life 35
What are You? 36
Train of thought 37
If I Died Tomorrow 39
Thank You 40
First Place 41
Observant 42

Smile 43
Blame it on the Alcohol 44
Beautiful Pressure Part 2 45
Wonder Woman 46
Will You Marry Me? 47
What if 48
D.O.C (Death of Cheater) 49
Skinny Jeans 50
What Every Woman Wants 51
Mz right 52
Addiction 53
Math 54
Perfect Aim Perfect Target 55
If I Died Tomorrow Part 2 56
Gold Digger 57
How to Make Love! 58
Breakfast at Tiffani's 59
Change 60
Colorful 61
Food for Thought Part 2 62

ACKNOWLEDGEMENTS

I act now because of you
I act now and pursue my goals
I act now because of what you told me who I can be, thank you God for the gift of writing
So I write as a present for the world to read
I appreciate you
I act now because I'm blessed living in these last days times are hard for everyone
I act now because of texts gmails emails aims and yahoo
I appreciate you
I act now simply because I acknowledge your sacrifice you made for me and money you gave to me
Children you and I made I appreciate you from state to state
Thank you Annie my heart my soul my wife, my kids Jayden and Kayla
Without you life seems joyless
My family, brother and sister roger and Christina my mummy who loves me no matter what
My father for his profound advice I acknowledge you
My close friends who helped me put my feelings onto paper and into action
Special thanks to Miss Iran for her words of wisdom and inspiration for me to write my book
Thanks Nesha, Shanel, Aaronay, Tatiana, Steph, Jordan and Chloe, thanks for giving me something that's free and can never be replaced your time
Thanks you Jite, Keara, Krista, Shalonda, Darlene, Lashanta, vena, much love from me to you
You are my escape to this madness in life
So many more friends who has had a impact in my life I acknowledge you to the fullest
My thoughts words ideas come from me to you and you to me last but not least I acknowledge me, no one can love me the way I will

Beautiful Pressure

Blue, pink, red, purple, yellow and green, what color diamond are you?
They say what does not kill you simply make's you stronger maybe that's why diamonds are forever
It takes courage composure little confidence and couture to be beautiful
It also takes carats color clarity cut and last but not least pressure to be a diamond
Great measure almost perfect timing, this is what puts a price on that rock
So what kind of diamond are you?
Like as if your mind is a mine the more you dig and search you will find that you are rare different breed raw but beautiful
Hidden in the darkness as if you sleep but before you wake up or shine there's some things you must meet face to face

Stress
Family
Relationships
Diseases
Work
Failure

All can cause pressure one way or another yet we all come from one mother
Like a diamond comes from the mother earth, the more you and I go through the more it shapes us makes us stronger into colors and cuts even leaving beauty marks

Optimistic
Pessimistic
Sexist
Blessed

What diamond shape has life molded you?

Round
Oval
Princess Cut, what are you?

However I don't wanna be judged by the size of my woman's butt
More what I do in my life when faced with pressure
Lies, truth, respect, chivalry, life & death, treat life like an office and front desk you
Some are full with clarity others say don't come near me
But we are all rare and priceless and expensive in our own special way
It's what you let people see & if you let them wear you out
So look for the inner diamond in you
I found mines on the corner of happiness and beautiful pressure

Good Morning

Can't sleep its close to morning
She lays beside me and starts mourning
Its time to head to the hospital
We stay calm, but the baby became hostile
As we enter the emergency doors
A weight lifted off me, she was in good care, but she's screaming get off me
Ready to proceed with the procedure, I said a prayer to God, I need you
For what seemed like a day & week, they let me in with full gear, when they was fully finish with groom and care
The sound beep beep from the monitor assured me she was here
With a head full of hair she felt fear
The doctor said here, I said right here
He said yeah, touched her ear
Held her from the rear and head
While I lay on the bed next to my wife I told her she looks like me right!?!
Speechless with a smile and a laugh
Kayla was born January 30th, 2009, what a way to start my new year.... took a while but she was here, took her small hands and said
Good Morning Kayla, daddy's here!!

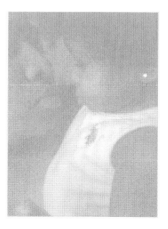

Goode Food for Thought

I used to front when I write poems . . . Talking about having nikes and ice on, when I can barely keep my lights on
I admit it, I did it, played the fool, played the station, I was EA SPORTS but God's creation
So I keep it real, real like swings in parks, real like stretch marks, real like monster inc under your bed when its dark wink
But now I'm good profound but still hood, at times, divorces the top loosen the strings what's really goode . . .
You have a name tag I have a tag name most people see the big picture I see the frame
Reset the game now I'm goode with a few changes . . . 2 women or 3 dimes and me looking at the sun my son . . . they all goode and that's what makes me feel like God with an extra 'o'
Now I have nikes on, no need to front on poems the only thing I front on is the front door to my home knock knock its confidence and he's feeling good
So I take insults as a complement, take it as a condiment, toiletry its BS to me it goes right past me right in the toilet you'll see, that I will always be happy see:) !!
Living life to the fullest no more rant and rave, learn to be like kanye and take the letter 't' up out the word can't . . . so next time you ask me how I'm doing I'll say I'm goode!!!
Let's face it no one wants to hear how I'm misunderstood

Disconnected

Sign in:

Password: word, I heard of technology but wow if I get twitter does that mean you will follow me see where I'm going and what I'm doing, who I'm pursing, who am I doing
What happen to cooing, real hug, baby how you doing? Human touch feeling for lust love in the eyes of your loved one, its gone downloaded no more fun so long
We don't laugh no more just type LOL . . . . where did we FELL type ohh where did we fall, treat the internet like a mall from one site to another looking inside go in send food and drink to one another . . . .
Treat our friends like sidekicks, some are ID and some LX kicks, black not black no more its blackberry . . . even Halle berry never did the Halle berry . . . . you tell me I'm confused
Use to getting used . . . we don't talk later on now it's BRB . . . what happen to a hug and pat on the back . . .
Saying goodbye . . . Start to cry, now we made upside down parentheses and lie dot dot dot but we not sad on our way in the train station or moving on the next lad
We get mad when people stare in our face, funny what you call MySpace nothing new just a new way for success, money for them for us stress
I'm just as guilty, guts full with lmao, you feel me? You miss me? you busy?
We use to say how we feel now we say blahhhhh I ain't had a kiss in a while all I get is muahhhhh
Mad when no one is online, mad when we online, but at the same time we waste time
Time online, America online, you should do the math I did . . . call me DMV I'm always online
It's hard to be real when we on the Internet, we gotta believe what they say yeah I bet, I'm giving you a taste of what you miss when you disconnect, no more walking into doors and cars etc . . . .
Do you know what I'm talking about? Wait don't answer I'm signing out . . . . click!!!

Gravity

Late bills due
Failing in school
No gas no heat
Rent goes up, check stays the same
Shoes starting to lean
Doormen being mean
Money ain't green, money is everything
Hope you don't have the swine flu
Silly kid questions "what did I do"
Silly women flexing "whose nu nu"
Silly man questions "what, who"!?!
Mirrors don't reflect just dissect who we are how we look
IPod, PSP, Nintendo DS, Blackberry's Iphones, Sidekicks, side chicks, replace books
Read magazines more than the bible
First sign of trouble asking God why you!?!
Battery dying sending last text
Bad customer service all you get is next
Fatherless, motherless children
She's a great grandmother and it's not cause of her children its cause she's a great mother
Single like a dollar, but nothing on her menu
Thinking to herself my kids eat first then you
Homes breakup cause of slutty earthquakes
Some things just can't be fixed
But better days ahead he said don't be mad at me
I'm just doing my job I'm Mr. Gravity!!!

Priceless

His and her perfect outfit for a night of bliss $500
Dinner for two under the moonlight at her favorite restaurant $100
Cuddle together at the movies sharing a buttery popcorn and large sprite watching old couples fight
On where they should sit as the movie lights dim like night $45
Yours and his favorite ice cream flavors on a cone on your way heading home $10
As she drops her ice cream while leaving the store he gives her his and says I don't want anymore
Wipes the cookies and cream mustache and holds her waste
Licks his fingers for the taste priceless
There are some things in life money can buy for everything else attention
It's priceless, never leave home without it

To Whom it may Concern

I thought I was next, but like fifth wheel I was just next
All those LOL's and smiles on text
Put on hold never got vex never had short hands deep pockets my complex was not a T-Rex
Meeting you I was blessed always here to talk hella positive
You was my YES now you like NO too busy, I gotta go, I just don't know I'm not sad just refuse to smile
Stop calling, pass your name refuse to dial
Like a light bulb looses fuse we will be here for a while or in the dark
Because I'm not feeling so alive it toned down like a file, I died awhile ago!
Cant say I gave up my heart but showed it to you, thought u was my doctor, thought we was popular
Knew how to operate, knew what to do but instead you made me cold lying on this table
We was so bible you know Cain and Abel, so now I'm able to sit up and now I blame myself I was small in your north pole world felt like an elf
We was never meant to be we just happened
I don't think you ever liked me, just like liking me because you have yet to put my heart back inside of me
Now I'm empty like building 9/11, me full of hopelessness and lust but I am sad maybe that's why they call it a crush, that's how I feel crushed I miss you this much
But where did I go left, what turn made it right did I give you a wrong signal put up a fight!
I must have and you make me crash and burn all is left is ashes spelled out
TO WHOM IT MAY CONCERN

I got so Much Better

Please don't complain to me, I am what I am you are who you was meant to be, be like Kobe and complain to the referee
I put on my smile lace up my confidence look in the mirror brush my compliment; button up my taste and style
Pull up my D.N.A because we all have different jeans
Wipe my sins away put in my pray say a prayer, then tom hanks cast away
I'm so torn between right and wrong left and bad up and sad down and happy
So I wipe my iPod off my face I tune into iTunes and walk to the base live and tone music is my life songs are my world so I like to fast forward my days and rewind my nights
Add to my favorites those days I put up a fight instead of giving up creating a playlist
I grew up, wise up, and got serious . . . .
Today these men are boys lack little of everything
Little confidence
Little romance
Little arrogance
Little game
Monday then two days later they little Wayne Guess they just Wednesday need to be Sunday's shine everyday
Everybody going hard, going in going this way going to win pregnancy rate is up
Somebody's cumin!
I'm wearing underwear on my head because I'm becoming cocky, went from maybe to possible to probably
Close my shutter and lay on my header fix my pillow I got so much better

My Friends Say

I'm Artistic
I'm Fly
I'm Stylish
But sometimes I don't see it
I'm kanyeezee
I have pure dopeness
I'm Magnificent
I'm fresh to death
I'm Sweet
But sometimes I don't see it
I'm real
I'm Amazing
I'm sensitive
I'm Popping
I'm Retro
But I still don't see it
I'm Poetic
I'm Awesome
I'm Original
I'm Lovable
I'm a Realest

I'm Kind hearted
But I don't feel it
This life mirror has no reflection of a positive altitude
It's how I feel inside so why lie be something I'm not although that's what they say I am
Now that's a Friendly Mirror

I Love You

She can be so cold sometimes
Then turn around and be hot
At times you make me sick, even rain on me with your tears
Turn my unsure yes to a not now that's a knot
So I tie a knot and walk all over you I'm so big apple that's what I always told her
But at the same time I respect you because you are beautiful
I started to like her more and more
As I got older I fell in love and never wanted to leave your side
We had our ups and downs and lonely nights cloudy skies summer nights
I lived in your lap while you took care of me from corner to corner, street to street
Always felt connected
You are full of lights, splendor and amazing to the eyes of the normal; everyone stares
at you and can't stop looking, take pictures and planes they booking
Brag they saw and met you even excited they was next to you, I'm not jealous though
This is no ordinary lady
I'm talking about NEW YORK my home
My true love, I love you

Who am I?

I'm not afraid of obstacles put in front of me
I bruise easy but never let that stop me
I hide my emotions and weakness to help me be great
I can be late but always there when you call; wow can you hear me now
I get up if I see a seat is in more need then me you know pregnancy, old lady
Try not to lie, cheat or steal just be honest, loyal, & willpower to do what's right
I'm clean cut in shape sometimes sloppy
Leave my underclothes on the floor
Not every day but weekends is a probably
I wear my success as a tie and love as a shirt use my jacket as Medal of Honor so I'm never hurt
Put on my belt of budget and pants of money because I wear the pants in this house
welcome to my honeycomb and my beautiful honey
My shoes are profound so I walk with substance
Ignore beautiful women but at times glance
Not perfect but I work it
I give and give until I can't any more
I put her to sleep Mr. Night Quill
Till she sore
I never want more, very content but won't settle for less in Lil Wayne life "I'm going in"
Shave my beard of ego so it can fly away
I'm a great father & a better husband
I am a MAN!!!!

Broken Thermometer

100 degrees but cold as ever broken so it tells her never say never
98 degrees she's too hot for anyone buttons up her affection ignores breeze of attention
80 degrees she angles her love like an ice cold glass of water cubes represent her children one cold mother
75 degrees she so in-between love vs. money
But stays out of sticky situations, hates to be called honey
55 degrees cold air has left so she goes right
Lifting weight with flirting its no longer a fight
49 degrees now she puts on her diva jacket
Looking for love still windy she had to pack it
35 degrees she's very hot ready to love
In her vocabulary is not the word money so she unknots her silk scarf and receive a kiss
20 degrees so ready to fall trip & dive into love
Afternoon texts saying you're the one I'm thinking of
15 degrees steamy feelings heat up ready to be felt up so her temperature rises, rises, and rises no longer nippy
Below 0 degrees she's sweating as he puts her to sleep, overheated not your average woman, she's different from other woman, pretty neat, pretty cool but very broken
Broken thermometer left as is, just promise you never open her
She's nuclear . . . . broken thermometer

The In-Crowd

Out and about, hard to catch me at home in and out my door is like "swing me alone"
My personality be like "leave me alone I'm fine on my medulla own"
I guess I was to small minded cause I just couldn't fit in
Like a shoe too small I just couldn't get in . . . . out of mix not bad just a batter
I have an abundant of friends some cool, some run game, I'm old school guess I'm just back pocket lame
In order and focused now I am, cause actions speak louder than words, and emotions get rebound
Pharrell I still can't see sound . . . .
Out right mad I left myself to be, did me
You know feel myself
And I don't mean tweet me
In happiness I was out and about again
Mr. Solodolo even though I still miss my best friend (young rich)
You more like where you been?
I'm more like how you been?
I said "around!!! Cause life is a circle so I square up and try every angle you know triangle . . . that's where I been
Let's just say I gave up on trying too fit in the: in crowd"

He Said She Said

He said "when you to tired to sleep that's when you know you tired"
She said "I treat rumors like a room, its empty until you put something in it"
He said "love is like quicksand the more you try to move and struggle out the more you fall deeper in"
She said "we all have disabilities some are visible and most are not . . . . so there should be handicap parking spaces in every ones parking lot"
He said "people that think they know it all is like a cup full of water, the more you pour the more they overflow with anger . . . sometimes you have to empty your mind to receive pure knowledge"
She said "if I told you how I feel you would not believe what you hear so I rather show you by my distance that way you can never feel me"
He said "life is like a Q-tip when you dig in the past all you get is dirty so . . . .

Q: QUIT
T: TAKING
I: IT
P: PERSONAL

The past is the past
She said: "they say life is a female dog so doesn't that make us the master
Always follow your dreams walk it feed it, pet it so when you sleep at night you still in reality because it's a dog eat dog world"
He said: "in a relationship a man will give his heart but a woman will give her ALL"
She said: trying is another way of saying I failed before I even start"
He said:" if we always fear what we don't understand we will never learn to grow as a person, as a result we may fall short as an individual"
She said: "A picture is worth a thousand words so if you want me expand your vocabulary and picture me"
He said: "Having faith is like holding onto a book with one hand, in time as each finger comes off faith becomes harder to hold onto
And eventually you let go, having a tight grip on reality is the only certainty for strong faith

So make sure those 5 things are of substance because that's how fast your 5 fingers let go of that book

She said: "Never say I changed my life, I did a 360 that just means your right back where you started

A complete circle"

Instead say I did an 180, that way you made a complete turn around about face now that's the right angle

He said: "You are like a shadow you can never pass me just get beside me or behind me"

She said: "I always tell the truth, even when I lie"

He said: "when it comes to confidence I try to puff puff pass, because if he's daddy I'm diddy take that take that"

Circus in Brooklyn

Come one come all
See the amazing denim
See that soft cotton
Come in walking leave out fly
More than just a store
More like a boutique
More than customer service
It comes with a greet . . . Smile, welcome
Tasteful style in many colors
My first time there, only response was
Those some fly brothers, where there wings?
Love their jeans, bags, shoes, ties, glasses, scarves, hats & elephants on every shirt
Brooklyn has never looked so colorful and critique
With a tent next to BK now that's neat
Admission is free to enter
Come spring, fall or winter
They just right oh so splendor
Come one come all there's a circus in Brooklyn
WELCOME TO BROOKLYN CIRCUS!

Mr. East Meets West

He went through the wire
I went through the fire, flames trials and tribulations
I went to summer school
He dropped out of college but still had a graduation, I rush through flashing lights he was patient
He said what I was always thinking
I stood still while everyone passed me
I just stood there blinking
He showed me to be myself despite what people think
I learned to bleed my words on paper use ink
I was profound he used singing dancing rapping sounds
He used music to touch me
So I put my hand out to meet him half way
I did more than hear I listened
He expressed himself even when they tried to diss him
Saw him twice met him once
Impressed he was, amazing so amazing
His performance, the way he came in
He was beyond hot he was Cajun
Glow in the dark tour I was watching
Live in direct he made me wanna be next to be a star
Months before that he signed my CD, shook my hand
I was spaced out and didn't wanna land he was fly sky high . . . . I can still hear him saying "get up and touch the sky!!!
He was fly
Without wings yes even sings . . . I'm east he's west
I'm nothing like them I feel blessed
In my life time Mr. East meets west . . . . Kanye west

FIRST AID KIT FOR DAUGHTERS

SHE GAVE BIRTH TO YOU SO ... AS A FATHER I ALSO HAVE SOMETHING TO GIVE
YOU
A FIRST AID KIT FOR DAUGHTERS
NOT FOR MOTHERS OR BROTHERS
SPECIALLY MADE FOR YOU
IT CONTAINS OVER 170 ITEMS BUT HERE'S JUST TO NAME A FEW
SPECIAL ALL PURPOSE INFORMATION IN NEED
PAIN, HURT OR DANGER
ALWAYS WEAR THIS NEVER TALK TO STRANGERS BAND-AID
SO YOUR HEART WON'T BREAK
IN CASE YOU FALL IN LOVE USE TYLENOL
WHEN YOU MEET A BOY WHO BOTHERS YOU AND BORING USE NEOSPORIN
NEVER LET A MAN DISRESPECT YOU IF HE DOES USE YOUR OMNIGLOW LIGHT
STICK
NO WORRY ITS NON TOXIC NOT FLAMMABLE
MEN CHEATING WEATHERPROOF ICE PICK
ICE PACK FOR WHEN YOUR DRESSES ARE TOO SHORT & TOO HOT
WHY NOT TAKE THIS EVERYWHERE YOU GO
IT HAS EVERYTHING IN THIS KIT FOR ALL BRUISES, FACES AND PLACES
BUTTERFLY CLOSURES, RUBBERS FOR COMFORT AND PROTECTION
YOU NEVER KNOW IF ITS YOU NEXTIN & ON TO THE NEXT ONE
YOU'RE MY BLESSING SO ITS ONLY RIGHT YOU ROCK AND ROLL
LIKE A BAND-AID KEEP YOUR LOVE ON HOLD
SHE GAVE BIRTH TO YOU SO ...
AS A FATHER I ALSO HAVE SOMETHING TO GIVE YOU!!!!!

Cranberry Juice and Grey Goose

The sun was set but no trees were blown
Just came from home out and about on a hot day
Felt like May with the a mix of June
Heading to an event that had a darkened room
Social buzz begin to fill the air
As I heard my favorite song here and there
I met cranberry juice with short hair
We mixed it well and drunk up that whole conversation forget anticipation I was feeling loose
Call me grey goose; time was going fast so we must have been having fun
Don't know what the ice breaker was
But my ice begin to break her down that day
Cold drink but warm topics found myself thinking
What can top this . . .
Purple, orange, grey and white who would have thought that night I'd have a colorful friend for life . . .
No more playing duck duck goose; there was a fuse light there . . . .
Left the scene with wishful thinking after a hug it had her thinking
What friendship would come of this, forget facebook we made our own chapter
Cranberry juice and grey goose the perfect mix, say ahhhh

Men's fitting room

Looking for the right cut, fit, size
Looking for that look in her eyes
Need to try her on so I take her in
She to small, I just can't fit in
Too many seams, pockets and style
I'm too big our relationship would only last a while
So I try another chick but she's too big ashamed what others would say "oh she's his"
I love her mountains but she fits me light valleys and high waters, too baggy not for me
Try on one last pair and they fit okay but I love the style denim and size
She could get in my pants any day
Women are like most men jeans, they don't last anyway
It's not them, there make or model it's his mind and who he follows
Can't keep his dipper in his zipper
So he will wear every woman out
To see what she's about
Keep the good pair to the side they can not get messed up she's too special
That's only for dress up
This is a man's dress code when it comes to women, spend half there life trying to fit in . . .
When all they have to do is try them on in the FITTING ROOM . . . .

Beautiful

Beautiful is more than looks, more than magazine's, more than books
Beautiful is not looking in the mirror but looking at it, passing it by
Beautiful is not pretty, amazing or cute
Beautiful is qualities that give great pleasure or satisfaction it's very mute
Beautiful is knowing not testing others of how beautiful you are
Beautiful is something that cannot be compared to money, life or cars
Beautiful is inside and out
Beautiful is scars and tattoos that tell stories
Beautiful is after a fight I walk past you and you can't ignore me
Beautiful is everyone in there own special way
So when someone ask you how you doing? Say
I'm beautiful and I'm gonna be the same the next day!!!!

Big Brother

Small house sleeping in a small room
Small conversation words spoken to soon
Hard on himself more hard on me on the basketball court we were the same size
running, passing, shooting
But somewhere, sometime, the ball lost air courts became full, time was running out,
between missed passes and shots & things changed
Small games, short names, he said you to small to play these big games
Always there until he got big
Big hopes & dreams but our conversation became foreign
I was his Scottie Pippen and he was Michael Jordan
Forget about little old me
Wonder if he knew I was the baby
He was too big to fit in my small world
He moved on to the next big thing money then a girl
Nobody's fault the love was there
Even though at times I felt he didn't care
Small house sleeping in a small room
He will always be my big brother
Even though he grew up too soon

Proud Son

For all those years, all your hard work I commend you for putting in work
Thank you for never giving up on me
Up at night late teaching me how to read, planting me, loving your seed
Saw the good in me and always positive
Miss optimistic willing to give
Two kids and a husband always time for me correcting my homework
Pressing your wet hands on my sheet
You cooked cleaned counseled critique, mom you was neat
On your worse day you was beautiful to me, mama's boy I was and was proud to be
I'm her boy she was all of me
A bond so tight I would die for her, but some where things changed I started to lie to her
Stopped expressing my feelings, feeling some sort of way
Broken compass lost my mommy, she still was there and ready with open arms when I found my way
Her voice was soothing very calm, showed me who's the master when she got her masters . . .
Success was born she got old but I grew up faster, married and distant from the love I needed
Our bond was unlocked we could not key it
If you was single I would marry you
If you was a leader I would follow you
Now I'm all grown now I feel I lost one, could not be everything you wanted
However I am a proud son

Pain

(inspired by MALIYAH JAYLA)

My attitude is tattoo so why change it rearrange it became something great
I loss something far more greater, bittersweet made me a hater so why change it
How can you love someone you never seen, I hate you because days go by you turn my eyes to gleam ...
Why change it
I hate to say it but we never met, there been days I leave my pillow wet, filled with pain don't call it tears
Call it years so I wipe the decade and dry my fear
When I hear your name I hear pain why change it
I like this feeling mixed with others wow its amazing, like finding my way in this maze guess I'm amazing
Taken away so fast, scared to look back ... no one can see there ass so I look past like I'm back in the future
Pain I feel but this pain shall heal in time like I'm stuck in a watch, just watch and hope no one ticks me off
So I aim for greatness where's my target eyes so red all I see is target, harder to get where I wanna go where I wanna be I feel pain and its cause of you lele
Priceless like a penny with a hole in it, touch my heart like I nicked you, you're my nickel
YOU WOULD HAVE BEEN MY DIME ... IT'S THE FOURTH QUARTER SO WHY CHANGE IT!!!!

Dumb It Down

In this continent my content makes me more confident but makes me feel self-conscious
So I dumb it down to your level, I hate what they tell you, I hate what they feed you,
food for though like they need you
We all say I'm gonna kill you, but you just be joking yet the dead speaks, someone dies
every other second talk about words spoken
I feel it's a drop back, when my personality drops back, people friends and family
take advantage of me
Funny is not funny when it's happening to you
But read magazines and newspapers like its something to do . . .
Talk about other lives and ours is messed up times two
We need not to dumb it down, but stay on the hilltop to be high toned
Speak up to be heard treat your conversation like a microphone
Word you don't gotta wear ecko to hear me
More think before we speak, teach before we preach, stop judging he's silly, he's neat
He's strong, she's weak, last time I checked we all was born with feet
I see a path to mark we all gotta walk in the street on the sidewalk
Welcome to Pathmark shop here shop there, shop everywhere
Last time I checked stupid tripped over ego and landed on gravity
Be smart not a clown
Raise the bar like a circus
And never dumb it down!!!

picture by Jordan Watson

Miss the Good Life

I miss the leaf green eye shadow rubbed on my v neck white tee
I miss the dirt smear on my sneaker toe stepped on so nicely
I miss the finger snap head roll as if you don't like me
I miss the bump on my back as you walk by me as if you don't like me
I miss the good morning good afternoon and goodnight me
So I put on make up not wearing my emotions on my sleeve hoping one day we make up, instead of run or leave
It's not like losing your key, more like losing apart of me
So heartless I'm blinded by flashing lights, I just wanted to be a champion and wanted glory
But you can't tell me anything, she made me stronger and I wonder this pain how much longer
I miss the good life now I welcome my self to heartbreak because all I see is street lights and bad news
When she said she will she was so amazing so amazing sometimes a Robocop and paranoid
But it was me who toyed with those emotions
I may have to move on she may never come around again until then I'm keep my love lockdown . . . . oh how I miss the good life!!!!!!

What are You?

May I have your attention please!
I am speaking in behalf of most if not all men on how I feel personally
We wanna know who are you?
What's the difference between a Girl Woman and Lady?
Personally I think there's a huge difference although we use these terms very loose
It seems it has made men lose also there respect, for who and what they want . . . so
I thought I would explain in my own words what each one means . . . .
A lady: To me a lady is someone not something . . . She's someone that has important goals and very outspoken but yet respectful
She is able to multitask and put her emotions and feelings aside in order to complete any task
She's driven and does not need a man to validate her . . . she's fly like an insect . . . beautiful like a lady bug
Likes to relax and on a nice day sit on the beach and lay
She's a LADY
A Woman: To me this puts you in a sex or gender, most woman dress in clothes tight enough to know they a women but loose enough to know they modest
They are outspoken love you to say how they feel, does not care about any ones feelings at times
They do everything a man can do and sometimes better, they strong smart and shine like a star
They wow any man in there sight . . . . They are a "wow a man"
She's a WOMAN
A Girl: To me this is associated with teens or a child someone who looks and acts like a kid
There immature and loud outspoken and think they are a woman and lady rolled in one . . . let people in there life easily
Have a need to feel wanted but soon puts up a wall that takes years to come down . . . they are there own worse enemy
However there also strong and very smart but have a hard time expressing it . . .
Can be shallow at times loves to wear name brand because there name is of no brand
You know like R.L (Ralph Lauren) and thinks she's a G.I Joe
Little do they know there not
She's a G.I-R L
She's a GIRL

TRAIN OF THOUGHT

AS I GET ON THE J TRAIN
MY MIND BEGINS TO WONDER
I GET A TRAIN OF THOUGHT
FIRST STOP, WORRIED, ABOUT GETTING TO WORK ON TIME, WHAT
WILL I EAT FOR BREAKFAST, HOW CAN I BE A BETTER FATHER
HOW ARE MY CHILDREN & IF THEY MISS ME
SECOND STOP, FOCUSED, ABOUT MEETING MY TASK AT WORK, SEEING
HOW EVERYONE WEEKEND WAS, MY SOFT HELLOS AND HARD WHAT
UPS TO CO-WORKERS, SAME OLD STORY MY WEEKEND SUCKS
WILL MY DAY GO FAST, HOW MUCH CASH IS IN MY POCKET, NEED TO
SAVE, MY FRONT DOOR DID I LOCK IT, DO I HAVE MY HOUSE KEYS
THIRD STOP, SIGHTSEE, ABOUT WHAT'S NEW
WHAT'S OLD, WATCH AS THE BUSINESS MAN FOLDS HIS NEWSPAPER
TO SEE WHO WON, HOW ABOUT THEM LAKERS
LATE KIDS FOR SCHOOL WATCH THEM RUN
MOTHER LOOKS TIRED, TELLS THEM TO COME
HOMELESS MAN ASK FOR CHANGE, SMELL IS TO MUCH TO BARE, BUT
THOUGHT OF ME BEING HOMELESS HAVE NO CHOICE BUT TO CARE
CHANGE TO DEEP SO I SAY A PRAYER
FOURTH STOP, HUMBLENESS, ABOUT TO GET UP AFTER MAKING
CONTACT WITH A PREGNANT LADY, MAYBE SHE NEEDED TO SIT MORE
THAN ME
MOVE TO THE SIDE AS PEOPLE COME IN, I WAS BUMPED, PUSHED,
STEPPED ON, BUT AS LONG AS THEY ALL IN, CONDUCTOR LETS MOVE
ON
AS THE DOORS CLOSE REMIND ME TO MOVE
MAKES MY EYES WONDER WHAT'S ABOVE YOU
FIFTH STOP, COMPREHEND, ABOUT WHAT I'M READING ABOVE
BILLBOARDS AND SIGNS
PARTY'S AND MEETINGS, WATCHTOWER'S AND AWAKE'S, COMMERCIAL
FLYER PITCH THEY IDEAS AS THE TRAIN ROCKS HERE AND THERE
SO I TAKE IN BOOK TITLES AND MAGAZINE TOPICS AS I STARE AT
ESSENCE LOOKING FOR A VIBE BUT ITS TOO COMPLEX
SO I WISH I WAS SEVENTEEN & HAD THE SOURCE BUT THIS IS THE
NEW YORK TIMES

IT'S ALL ABOUT THE BLACK HAIR & MAKEUP TIPS & DOUBLE XL
I'M READING IN A SLOW SET
LOOKS LIKE IT'S MY STOP TIME TO JET
SIXTH STOP, JAY STREET, WHERE MY MIND IS AT EASE, ITS LIL HOOD
LESS THANK YOU'S, YOUR WELCOMES & PLEASE
IT'S MY STOP TIME TO GET OF CHECK FOR EVERYTHING I'M SO PLAIN
BUT FEEL LIKE I'M FLY, TIME TO TAKE OFF
THE STREETS IS MY RUNWAY SO I WALK TO THAT BEAT ALREADY IN
THE STREET
TIME FOR A NEW DAY, BUT I NEVER LOOSE MY TRAIN OF THOUGHT
BECAUSE I DO THE SAME THING EVERYDAY

If I Died Tomorrow

Have breakfast with my family, talk about good old days driving that 96 Camry sitting in the back seat as a child
Do a little shopping for me and those I love give them something to remember me by when I say bye
Have my afternoon with my kids
Show them things I could never see again
Give them a crash course on facts of life, that way they turn out steady remain neutral always in gear
Never reverse always driven and turn towards right, stay away from wrong and park there success
Tell my friends things I could never say on text or email give the phoneless friends my cell
Have my night with my wife tell her see you later because I hate goodbyes
Hold her tight as if I'm stopping her from a fight . . . .
Show her instead of telling her, keep her in sight that's some insight
We would name our days
Call tomorrow better call today it will be
So each day is a message
I want this to be the day after yesterday . . . so I can live it all over again
But its said and done I'm her zero she's my number one, sorrow slapped pain and death broke up the fight . . .
What a night . . . if I died tomorrow

Thank You

Welcome to my world please enter where emotions are a accident like a fender bender
Welcome to my life where joy and sadness rain
Welcome to umbrella of protection fame
Don't have to be famous to be a star just shine so every often like a star
Welcome to my affection that fly past your man
Welcome to a friendship that will sail away
Over the love down below, that old school peanut butter and jelly time flow so PB
This ship has many places to go from a friendship to a relationship
Pray for no wind of hardship so we can dock safely, your so nautical
Guess I'm crazy
I Guess what I'm trying to say is thank you and your welcome!!

First Place

I want to win this race in life
I want to be next, wipe my life away Windex it next it
So I treat my thoughts and feelings like a Lego set build it up to the sky and let go
I'm so fly I can see tomorrow and the day after yesterday
So call me Mr. Back to the future because I got a lot of jigga watts, call my wrist the zoo because all my g shock bathing ape do is watch
Keep looking straight as if my life is on the light yellow, I'm light speed, like speed, mix a little Carmelo
They say hey to you but to me they say hello I'm bright nice
Which means I'm light skin which means I like a light skin rapper say lil Wayne . . .
I'm going in because I dread this he may be the ish but I'm getting nasty, I mind as well be piss because I piss off any one I pass in life
I'm in first place for now, seeing how long this last . . . Everyone knows how to run but not everyone knows how to crash!!!

Observant

I observe her walk, as she moves side to side; she's a planet rotating around me
Her curves are outta this world, I wanna get beside me so I can look at the space and see what she looks like beside me . . . .
I observe her moonwalk, as she walks on the moon, I'm so attentive I notice everything
The color shadow over her eyes, matches her mood ring which is covered by her bag handle
Them jeans sing, must be her D.N.A, BUT SHE AINT WEAR THEM YESTERDAY
That's a different fade, style, she's a classic my anti drug and coke
She's gonna be here for awhile she's dope
I observe her mole on her back, not her dough and where it goes
I know how she smells, she smells like she's mine
Her bracelet watch doesn't even tell time
Loves lemon hates lime, she's so sprite, and I'm so mountain dew
Dumped Dr. Pepper because all he talked about was what he do
She's an insect she has no backbone, she's a star living alone but she shines so bright
Loves her dress it's not black its night; shoes looks like the street
So she walks the nights flashing lights
I observe the way she reads on her lips slowly move
Her hair color reminds me of food
Loves those streaks call them "chicken cordon blue"
Those other dudes belong in the alphabet
They you're X . . . you told me they Gatorade cause they always ask "is it in you" when yall have sex
I'm next up I'm taking off
I'm observant; I'm fly cause I'm off the wall can't wait to beat it

Smile

If I told you, you're beautiful would you smile
The way your eyes look in pictures
It shines but tells a story, it figures
From your curves to your neutrons in your brain
If I told you that you're rare, smart, sheer like see through but hard to tear
One of a kind breed of your own no clone
A woman transformed into a lady
That's a butterfly flying above all, your so Jill Scott, so Beyonce, okay
Does it make you smile to know you're admired by every man on earth?
You're out of this world what boys' dream, funny you're what I'm dreaming of, climb mountains high as the Palisade's Mall
I think your amazing does that make your smile

Blame it on the Alcohol

She says she miss me
Proves it by giving me that cat, so in the end I'm pulling hair from my teeth
That's what I call strong whiskey
When I'm tired I'm at lost for energy but ill settle for a blow job if she tempts me
She loves my long island ice tea so I lick her moscato while she watches TNT
Try to follow, go full court till tomorrow till we fall asleep and awake from that bay breeze
She ask me if I ever had sex on the beach, I told her no but I love sand ill watch if you teach
She so cosmopolitan, her shoes are so politician they talk to me
I love her body, lips like strawberry skin like a daiquiri
As she moves her hips her body shakes like jello shots now that's one sweet bitch
However she needs work maybe a screwdriver
So when I'm upset I tell her I'm gonna kill her, but she makes me fall for her she so tequila
I feel her she feels me relationship is still at times amaretto sour
You know rusty nail
But she worth the try I'm gonna give it a go and rum and coke she's no red head slut more like bloody mary yum
So I give her the old tomato and then the ultimatum
I'm no blue lagoon and I don't play the fool more like a mojito
She can be very brandy sweet like kandi so I over look her flaws, we mix it like gin cause we so confident
As I hold her hands pretty nails like French pina colada tips
We watch the tequila sunrise because we was meant to be but I refuse to blame it on the alcohol

Beautiful Pressure Part 2

350 thread count lays across a king size bed
Its about 50 degrees in the bedroom
Her goal is to make him come soon
His job is to turn that room into June
Hot sweaty wet and wild
As he eats her up
She so loud he tells her to shut up
With a mouth full of her he continues to taste test
Treats her body like bus stops, next
He licks, bites, pulls, and kisses
Goes over and over for the spots he misses
She's a diamond in the ruff
And likes it ruff
How else will she shine unless he's tuff?
So he becomes Reggie and goes for the bush
He's no longer a saint once again says shhhhhhushhhhhhh
She's grabbing the sheets off the bed other hand holding his head
Biting her lip, that's his tip so he knows to go deeper
Grip of the sheets gets weaker says to herself this diamond is a keeper
Beautiful pressure she begins winning
Beautiful pressure perfect timing
Beautiful pressure he doesn't mind she's a diamond!!!!
Rare cut, shape size and in his eyes she's perfect
He makes her come first then he arrives later
He does what he does & puts her to sleep
Beautiful pressure as he awaits for round three'
Says to himself "she's a princess cut to me"

Wonder Woman

Climb the ladder in fashion, miss independent never asking
Has grown from girl to woman to lady
Ready for any obstacle, only believes what's proven with ocular proof
Never selfish more like shoes and dresses and aquarium colors fish
Hair on point, other chicks is exclamation points and question mark she glows in the dark
Strong mentally emotionally and sexually, weak for love men and chocolate
Built for tuff body is a winter wonder land
Cold on the outside warm on the inside
Personality can be stormy with a cloudy chance of attitude
Never nice but have respectful latitude rather give then take she does not sit at home she's not silicone or fake!!!
Very real definition of a lady wild at times but less crazy
God is her numerator everything else is her denominator
When she leaves, she's not coming back you are your own terminator
Does not mind when you come onto her what you give is what you get she's very karma
You think she's sexy, but she thinks she Pepsi
Shaped beautiful however a classic yet cold and can be messy blessed you are to have met a real woman rare breed . . . . I don't wonder I know I got a wonder woman!!!

Will You Marry Me?

I don't know how to say this as the housewarming got colder
But this is my last thing to do on my to do may list
Its almost June and I know you steady but I'm ready to be your broom
I wanna sweep you off you feet if you let me
I want to make you special because your limited edition
Last beautiful woman on earth, and I want you to myself
They say men are from Venus and women are from mars
I think that's so not true because you are my star
You were far far away but my love found you
Did not hear the alarm so I snoozed on our love and now I'm late
Just wanna meet you at love: 30 one date even though I'm 2 min past attention
Quarter past affection, hope I'm not a second from rejection
I know you on to the next "him"
But before your new man comes back
I have to get on one knee, I have a question . . . .

What if

If I was a woman
I would not want children
If I was a woman
I would be pulling not pushing
Cash money would be my focus
Behind life, family & God first
I would want a lot, before I pull out in a hurst
If I was a woman
I would desire nothing less than greatness
Tell my man when I want him or need him
Actions speak louder than words
But in reality I hear words as if they screaming
That's just me
If I was a woman I would be sexy by what I do not what I wear
Different me everyday new style
New hair
Have a female clic, dress somewhat alike
Have one male close friend we would be tight
Calm my man down when he upset
Run up his bath water set dinner
Treat him like a champ my winner
If I was a woman
I would be one of a kind blind to dudes
Make up my own rules
My makeup would make you wanna be first to makeup before a bad breakup
If I was a woman I would take the good with the bad never show it
Hold it let it out in private
It's my relationship I'll throw it over board in private
What if I was a woman?
I think it would make me a better man

D.O.C
(DEATH OF CHEATER)

LA LA LA LA HEY HEY HEY GOODBYE
I MUST STOP WITH THE 100 BUDDIES ON AOL AIM
I MUST STOP THE HALF TIME SHOWS STOP WITH THE GAMES STOP WITH THE HOES
I MUST STOP WITH THE PHONE ON SILENT
THIS IS DEATH OF A CHEATER, MOMENT OF SILENCE
I MUST STOP FLIRTING, ALTHOUGH HARD TO GET PAST THERE SMILE, BUT HATE TO SEE HER FROWN
DRAWN ON HER FACE I'M MAKING HER A CLOWN AND SEE WHO I'M HURTING
I MUST STOP HAVING MY CAKE & EATING IT TOO, BUT IT'S MY FAVORITE FROSTING WHAT'S A MAN TO DO
I MUST STOP LIES, AND UNTRUE COMPLIMENTS
THERE'S A THIN LINE BETWEEN FLIRTING & A COMPLIMENT
I MUST STOP THE SNEAKING IN WHEN ITS DEAD SILENCE
I MUST NOT WORRY WHAT OTHERS ARE THINKING, WHAT MATTERS IS WHAT'S SHE'S THINKING
I MIGHT CHANGE THE WAY I DRESS
TONE IT DOWN, EVERY ANSWER CAN'T BE YES, GOT TO SAY NO
TIRED OF THINKING WHO SEEN ME IN THAT TOYOTA OR CAMRY
NEED TO START THINKING ABOUT MY FAMILY
BUT I WON'T BE IN MY GIRL FACE ALL DAY
TALKING ON FACEBOOK LIKE I BE IN MY GIRL FACE ALL DAY
A REAL WOMAN DON'T GOTTA BE IN FRONT OF YOU TO SEE OR SENSE SOMETHING WRONG
BUT THIS IS MY CHANGE MY TUNE MY SONG
NO NEED TO MUTE, TURN IT DOWN TO PURE SILENCE
THIS DEATH OF CHEATER, MOMENT OF SILENCE
TOOK A KNIFE OUT AND KILLED MY SWAG
LET OUT A SIGH
LA LA LA LA HEY HEY HEY GOODBYE!!!

Skinny Jeans

Who's to say what's beautiful & fit
Like there's a definition for that one word
Plus we all come in different shapes & sizes
Plus sizes are looked upon different
But there's no difference
As long as we get over that fence hence
I don't have skinny jeans or wear them
My DNA needs more room more space so I'm more fly I'm galaxy
spaced out
It seems my seams are better not to confuse cocky with
confident
We both have some things in common like being a go getter
But never be ashamed of your size
You are what you are, in time we get better, like wine
Skinny or large we all got zippers, front & back pockets
Difference is we carry rockets they just got missiles skinny
jeans
Same tissues with issues
When God made you He blessed you
So carry on like a carry on
To your desired plane
At the end of the day only God can judge our weigh in

What Every Woman Wants
(Inspired by Lady A)

You want to be somebody's everything
The warm feeling when they touch you, when they kiss you
When they say your name
You want to be someone they will always remember and couldn't forget you even if they tried
You want to find your best friend and someone you can tell all your secrets too
No matter where they are they always see a little bit of you in everything
A guy who wakes up in he middle of the night and sends you a text just because he thought of you
When he is with you all he can do is look in your eyes and tell you nothing but the truth because he knows how much lies hurt you
Be honest even if it hurts, when you fight he's the first to say sorry because the thought of you being mad at him kills him
Someone you can take your anger out on and he doesn't take it personal because he knows you didn't mean it
Someone who can look at you when you just wake up in the morning and say god you're beautiful
Not someone perfect just someone real
The kind of love that makes you wish he didn't have friends
The kind that make you selfish, makes you needy because all the time in the world just isn't enough anymore
You want the inside jokes everyone gets annoyed about, you want to feel like you belong to him, believe that there is someone out there who has so much chemistry with you its mind blowing

Mz right

Beautiful inside and out knows what Houston Texas is about
Peaceful when it comes to love and war hates milk, at times attitude is sour
Sometimes funny mostly mean her drive was so driven she could be a ford focus
More of a close friend as time went on, conversation became tall very long
Friendship got strong, she could do no wrong
Said what was needed to be said texted what needed to be texted
There was no in between it was always no or yes
She was hard, hard body hard as wood, but I had that fire created a flame and burning sense of pride
So insightful so in light she was glowing
I admire her because of what she's been though and where she is going yes she is still glowing
In the dark
Beautifully made butterfly
Friends to bestie too family
Mz right can do no wrong left to me

Addiction

I have an addiction more less fiction
So I treat attention like a puzzle to see what I'm missing
I have an addiction baby maybe you can smile like this where your heals like that
I have an addiction love the way your heel sits in that baby phat shoes
I have an addiction with kissing confidence we will have a baby and name her complement
I have an addiction it's admitting
Sometimes being honest I'm just kidding to others I'm hitting
Last time I checked there's only one soccer ball but everybody's kicking they so NOT David Beckham they goals they missing bad aim no target they get red . . . It's because they hear but don't listen that's there
Addiction

Math

See the problem is I can't find the answer
My whole body starts to shake as if I was struck with cancer
My life plus the stress starts my test of faith
So I use addition and add material things, walk around as if I'm a king
However all these things don't equal a Queen
So I divide my thoughts and see how many things I can fit into my day
We all know 24 hours in a day can turn your no's into okay's now that's overtime
Still not enough time in a day, does not add up until payday and we still need more
So I subtract my problems and people who cause pain take away from things wanted for the things needed
Try not to get heated on, but cool down just because we see a circus don't mean we gotta be a clown
We all know God is to the second power and can multiply our blessings
The problem is we always guessing
Never finding a solution which causes confusion
Wrong answer wrong man wrong questions like is this where I stand?
Wrong way on how to treat a man I see
Men have they hands on there woman ... Weeks go by see a full pack of tampons in the cabinet wonder why they not used feeling scared abused
Where did they go wrong?
He multiplies he's a dad needs to be a father ... You know hands on
Like how your hands were on in the beginning you what's missing
I'm not good in math but good in life treat it like a bike one foot at a time look straight ahead never down
Turn to where you wanna go stop when you need to and go pass those who pretend like they need you
As life goes on it gets fast so sit enjoy the ride you will be surprised the answer you find!!

Perfect Aim Perfect Target

Boy: Hey ASL, what kind of cell
Girl: 21, female, earth Nextel
Boy: I like send pic
Girl: I sent 3 take your pick
Boy: I love all, your sexy send more
Girl: Okay sure but let me see you
Boy: see me, what it do?
Girl: I like too ohh send more too
Boy: We should meet like a date
Girl: Why not we live in the same state
Boy: okay talk to you later xoxo
Girl: Blushing this night gets better & better
Sign off door closes, behind an online door who knows this danger lurking
What's suppose to be a boy is really a man Sam is 42
Knows what to say what to do prey on the weak & opened minded . . .
Timed it, watch her in a chat room waiting to attack
Mom & Dad should have took that laptop back
Under age, under influence, inexperience
He saw her as bait
Little does she know it's her last date
Lack of parent advisory, spamless, too wireless, careless, she will be used very useless
He's a predator, likes girls who they think they hard to get, little do they know
He has perfect aim perfect target!!!!
800,000 juveniles (under 18) are reported missing each year

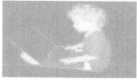

If I Died Tomorrow Part 2

Hangers stopped swinging
Doors no longer close & open
Things would have been odd
Changed like metro to a token
Wishing turned into hoping
One side of the bed colder
Son & little girl survived with no male figure to mold her
This is that love story that hates to be told
How it must unfold page by page it's a house no longer a home
Stale cologne
No more love making
Affection bringing flowers to depression's reception
She can't come find him, only God she can confide in
She looks through her window as a widow
He would want her to carry on, use his pillow
No more forward texts, emails or pokes on facebook
No more "enough shopping I'm tired" look
Words of endearment is on vibrate small as a be buzz
As she thinks about what he called her she shakes
True reality wishes it was fiction
Her man she is missing
Kissing his pictures, reading old texts, no's and yeses
Treats every morning new pushes play
Can't rewind or pause just TiVo her favorite memories
Just a bunch of, remember me's
If I died tomorrow things would not be the same
Hangers would stop swinging
Doors would stop opening & closing
Things would have been odd, changed from a metro to a token

Gold Digger

She gives it up for that handsome face
She gives it up for that nice body like oh he can ride me I'm focused like a ford
She gives it up for the money & security; he got money to blow so she can shop instead of work
In her head it's plenty she so fendi
She gives it up for the love, because he said he loves her
But she doesn't give it up
She's a gold-digger, with her mental shovel she digs for the right man
Love vs. money soft words spoken when she says honey, free hugs and kisses
But no hits until she misses
She's looking for gold because her body will blow your mind kind of like finding gold in a mine
When she gets her accounts and have serious money you will taste that honey
As you come up for air, she will be laughing all the way to the bank
Now that's funny money

How to Make Love!

please follow these ingredients
1 tablespoon of attention
½ cup of rubbing oil
1 bed
500 thread count of Egyptian cotton
3 teaspoons of kisses and hugs
¾ of feelings and affection
Mix until hot and bothered then let stand
Stir in some more of you and put in oven
Watch and let it rise
Insert a few inches in to see if done and moist
Turn the heat up to 350, ask if you miss me
Take out let it cool
Enjoy your love, repeat until need is met
This may cause pregnancy & addiction of one another and may be hot caution

Breakfast at Tiffani's

Hi sir may I take your order?
You can tell she fly like a plane
You can find her in white plains
Other places come close but just not the same
So they JET, afraid to get near cause she so fear
You can see her beautiful design, inside & out
Directions could not even help you out
Hard to find she's precious as
Time so once you loose her you never get her back
She's a quarter past a dime
You're just late
You have to navigate your heart & soul
Even though she's hot she can be cold
Engine for a brain ferrari for her body frame
So she serves a appetite for destruction, upset stomach from loving these brothers just bluffing
No spine they fronting ain't that something
Heartburn from letting it burn, too much
Concern so she season life with learn
Which means her love has to be earned, savored
Order what you want, eat what you need meet her to see if you like her meat
She's tasty smell like "taste me" she so pastry you maybe she certainty
So I tip tiffani miss they ant got nothing on me
She can close her eyes and create a epiphany make you eat up her attention digest her flaws and all
You will always want more but remember this place is secluded
And no tip included

Change

There are two sides to a dime, one that gets ahead and one that tales behind
Never mind what you thinking its better to know, most rejections is followed after a NO
Doors are shut options are closed all to because you tried to get to close to designer clothes
Want nothing when we have money not even hungry
But be dead broke and just change or a twenty
But that's when we want it the most when we hungry the most
It's does not matter if you carless homeless jobless phoneless its worse being necklace no back bone or spine not that's spineless
Dreams is something high that we must reach so we associate it with clouds because we have doubts
We hope because we can't hop so we pray, we never stop doing what ever it is we are doing
In life we don't get adidas just Nike so we check backwards and hope the three stripes or strikes don't come back and bite me
So keep your head up and your neck straight your eyes for sight to see the daylight
And if you stress sleep on it that's why God gave you night
Sometimes change is good

Colorful

It seems we living the American dream which is more then what I have seen for myself
We can't say we was better off before
Before we wanted more now they give us less I think as black people we never had it so how can we be mad we was always in a recession it just had a mask on called depression
It seams we care more about what we wear then where we going
I am guilty just like Nike I just do it
Its always if and but or more . . . . can't settle always want more to impress who
Last time I checked we all wore flesh dude
Men want a woman with curves and they a broken road
Woman want money but yet have no where to hold it pot to piss in
Chilled with a baller talking bout I'm going in
But get traded at the end of the season after a championship win
It seems I'm mad but just sad wondering why we can't change
One person cannot make a difference however a difference can make a change in one person
No matter the color black or white
At the end of the day we are all night!

Food for Thought Part 2

I wake up
Sit up
Get up
I don't slip up
But I'm so tall I fall short
No we fall short
I think we fall short so we can learn to pick ourselves back up
We loose touch with our English so we say
What's up
We fall in love because we to busy trying to make sure we don't trip up
We cheat on life diet's and friendships because we afraid we may give up
I say we because I'm speaking about you and me
We think up is good and down is bad, wishing what we had what we want when right in front of us is what we need
It doesn't take a broken heart to know it bleeds so we should stop the hate and realize from young what we was taught I speak the truth so this is
Food for thought!!

Made in the USA
Columbia, SC
08 November 2022